It's A Mystery,

Charlie Brown

Charles M. Schulz

Random House · New York

Library of Congress Cataloging in Publication Data

Schulz, Charles M   It's a Mystery, Charlie Brown.   "A Charlie Brown special."   I.   Title.
PN 6728.P4S32   741.5'973   74-24523   ISBN 0-394-83101-2   ISBN 0-394-93101-7 (lib. bdg.)

Manufactured in the United States of America   1 2 3 4 5 6 7 8 9 0

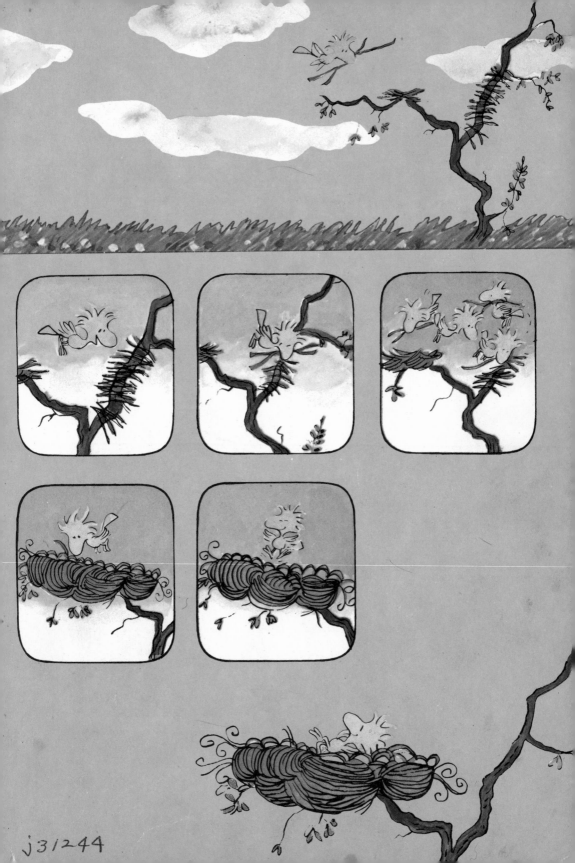

I'm doomed. I'm doomed.

What's the matter, Sally?

She's out to get me!
She's out to get me!

What are you talking about?

My science teacher. Every week she makes me bring in a new exhibit. I'm going to have a nervous breakdown before I'm six years old!

Well, I don't see what the . . .

This week it's got to be something from nature. Why don't we leave nature alone? It's not bothering *us!* Why do we have to bother *it?*

Now, look, Sally . . .

But I'll show her. I won't crack. I refuse to crack. I'll get the best exhibit she's ever seen!

Good grief!

*Some stupid person
has stolen my nest!

Your nest is missing, you say?

Fear not, little friend....

I, *the great detective, will
solve this mysterious case.*

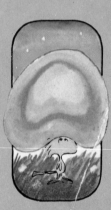

What's going on here? What are you doing?

Why are you giving me the third degree?

A nest? I don't know what you're talking about. What nest? I haven't seen any nest! I refuse to confess to something I don't know anything about.

Dusting for fingerprints!
He's finally flipped!

He's gone crazy! Linus, stop
him! Stop him! He's going to
ruin the house!

Cough!

Cough!

Ahg!

Ashes to ashes and dust to dust. Snoopy will find it,
and find it he must!

Ah-hah!

That's a broom straw.
So what?

Ashes to ashes and dust to dust.
When there's a problem, in Snoopy we trust!

If that beagle can
find anything, I'll be
very surprised.

Ashes to ashes and dust to dust.
The proof of the pudding is under the crust!

Ahghhh!

I don't understand, sir.

I don't understand you, sir.

You don't make any sense, sir.
Good night, sir.

Snoopy! How are you? It's so nice of you to drop by to see your old friend, Pig-Pen!

How have you been?

Nice talking to you. . . . Come again! I don't have too many visitors!

Snoopy! What a surprise!

What in the world are you doing?
Is this some kind of game?

Hey, cops an' robbers! Great!

Stick 'em up!
Bang! Bang! I gotcha!

Boy, I like cops an' robbers. Wait here—I'll be the robber, okay?

Okay, Sherlock. . . . Now
I'll hide and you find me.
Okay?

All right, copper.
Your money or your life,
you dirty rat!

You lily-livered copper!
You'll never take me alive!
No one's taking me in!

Hey, kid! Come back! We didn't finish the game!
Come back, Snoop!

I've been robbed!
I've been betrayed!
Somebody's out to get me!

Now what?

I brought in the best exhibit in my entire first-grade career. Somebody stole it. Get my lawyer! Get my bookkeeper!

What *was* your exhibit, Sally?

A prehistoric bird's nest. Do you understand how valuable that is? Get my accountant! Get my...

What do you mean, prehistoric?

I found a nest that was so ridiculous it had to be prehistoric. No self-respecting modern bird could have built it.

Sally, you took Woodstock's nest! That's terrible! Snoopy and Woodstock were up all night looking for it.

I demand justice! I demand restitution!
I found the nest and the nest belongs to me!

I want my nest back! I demand
you give me back my exhibit!

Now, look, Sally, I don't want you to fight with Snoopy and
Woodstock. Let's settle this in a civilized manner. Let us find an
objective person to settle this.

We have a dispute to settle here, Lucy. Perhaps you could help us solve the problem? A matter of establishing ownership. . . .

It's a legal matter, then?

Yes.

You've come to the right place.

O yes, O yes. The court is now in session. The stenographer will please take down all events pertaining to this case.

Seven cents, please.

But you haven't done anything yet!

Okay, I said court was in session. Present your case.
I haven't got all day!

I found a bird's nest,
and it's mine.

Hold it, hold it! Bird,
do you have someone to
represent you?

Snoopy?

And you, Sally Brown. Who is representing you?

I'm acting in my own behalf.

All right, let the blame rest on whom the court decrees.

You, bird, state your defense.

To the court ...
Whereas the party of the first part, hereafter known as Woodstock, and whereas the party of the second part, hereafter known as Sally Brown—therefore and heretofore were, are, and will be parties to or therefrom to this agreement ipso facto quod ist landum and whereas in subsequent parties of value and pluribus cum laude; therein and hereto ...

Oh, good grief!

Now, you, Sally Brown, state *your* case.

I say, finders keepers,

losers weepers!

A very strong case
indeed! Hmmmm!

THE JUDGE

Stenographer, please read back the plaintiff's last statement.

Uh . . . uh . . . actually I just got past the "O yes, O yes," and . . . then, uh. . . . What came after "O yes"?

Good grief!

Hmmmm. . . . Let's see. . . . You said, "ipso facto," and threw in a "pluribus cum laude. . . ."

And you said that stuff about "weepers." . . . Hmm.

The court finds in favor of . . .

. . . the bird! Bird, it's your nest. Keep it.

I've been robbed! I'll appeal! I'll take it all the way to the Supreme Court!

Another such outburst and I'll clear the court. Court is adjourned!

I'm ruined! I'll get a failure on my experiment. This does it. My career grinds to a halt before I even get started.

Don't worry, Sally. Maybe we can help. We'll see what we can come up with.

I don't care if you *have* thought about it all night, Charlie Brown! I still won't do it!

But it's the only thing to do. It'll be a good experiment.

I don't even know who the man *is!*

But Snoopy says he'll do it. And if he's willing to do it, *you* ought to be.

Oh, all right. I'm stuck. I have to do something. But if the class laughs at me, I'll never forgive you.

For my science exhibit, I want to talk to you about Ivan Petrovich Pavlov. Who is he, you ask? I will tell you. He is a great Russian doctor. He studied our nervous system.

And do you know why we have a nervous system? So we can get nervous making these stupid reports. . . . Yes, ma'am . . . I'm sorry, ma'am.

Anyway, he did a very famous test once with a dog. He wanted to prove a dog could drool if you rang a bell and promised him food. What? How do I know this? Somebody just told me.

Anyway, I will now recreate that famous experiment.

As they say, all's well that ends well. I got an A on my exhibit, Woodstock got his nest, and Snoopy got a little attention.